C000227848

The FABRIC QUANTITY HANDBOOK

FOR SOFT FURNISHINGS

MERRICK & DAY

The
Fabric
Quantity
Handbook

A CIP record for this book is available from
The British Library.

ISBN 0 9516841 7 5

Printed and bound by Butler & Tanner, Frome, England

Merrick & Day
Southfield, Redbourne, Gainsborough,
Lincolnshire DN21 4QR England

Telephone +44 (0)1652 648814
Facsimile +44 (0)1652 648104
e-mail merrick.day@drapes.u-net.com
Web site: http//www.drapes.u-net.com

The
FABRIC
QUANTITY
HANDBOOK

FOR SOFT FURNISHINGS

Catherine Merrick
and
Rebecca Day

MERRICK & DAY BOOKS AND PATTERNS

THE ENCYCLOPÆDIA OF CURTAINS

Packed with inspirational full-colour photographs, over 600 clear line
diagrams and step-by-step instructions, this is an indispensable curtain-
making guide. With graded projects, from quick and easy to elaborate
swags and tails, many techniques are explained here for the first time.
A wealth of experience in one book.

THE CURTAIN DESIGN DIRECTORY *THIRD EDITION*

A manual of black and white illustrations, with over 300 design ideas for
curtains and soft furnishings. Complete with new easy-to-use Style Guide
to identify quickly the appropriate window treatment for any situation.
The twelve sections include Design Details, Poles, Valances, Bay, Tall and
Narrow and Problem Windows, Beds and Accessories. The ultimate guide
to the creative world of window treatments.

THE SWAG AND TAIL DESIGN AND PATTERN BOOK

Everything you need to make beautiful swags and tails in one book.
Over 70 swag designs to choose from, supported by make-up notes and
full sized swag and tail patterns. Complete with tracing paper to copy
patterns from the Master Pattern Sheet.

SUPPLEMENTARY SWAG PATTERNS

To complement The Swag and Tail Design and Pattern Book, this Master
Pattern Sheet contains eight swag patterns graded in size up to 170cm
(67in) wide. The patterns and tracing paper are presented in a wallet.

PROFESSIONAL PATTERNS FOR TIE-BACKS

Patterns for plain, banana and scallop-shaped tie-backs each in 8 sizes.
Clear step-by-step instructions. Presented in a wallet with tracing paper.

Mail order service available from

Merrick & Day Orders Department
Southfield, Redbourne, Gainsborough DN21 4QR England
Tel +44 (0)1652 648814 Fax +44 (0)1652 648104
email: merrick@drapes.u-net.com
Web site: http://www.drapes.u-net.com

All books subject to availability

CREATIVE CURTAIN COURSES

MERRICK & DAY run a range of curtain-making courses in their
Lincolnshire workroom. They are based on practical tuition
and offer a wealth of professional hints and tips.

CONTENTS

How to use this book

This book is designed to make the task of estimating fabric quantities for curtains, accessories and trims easier and more accurate. The tables have been formulated as the result of our experience making bespoke soft furnishings. However, when estimating for specific designs, the quantities given may need to be adapted and so should only be used as a guide.

Allowances

The fabric quantity calculations take into account seam and side turning allowances. Standard allowances for gathered curtain overlaps and curtain and valance return measurements have been deducted to give the track or pole and pelmet board or valance rail sizes.

The measurements have been rounded to the nearest 5cm and assume a pair of curtains.
The curtain, valance and Austrian blind tables have been calculated on three different fullness ratios – 2, 2¼ and 2½. Choose the most suitable fullness ratio for the type of heading to be used.

The calculations are based on the following allowances:
1.5cm seam allowances
6cm for side turning
2 x 7cm overlaps for curtains (7cm for actual overlap and 7cm for ease)
2 x 8cm returns for curtains
2 x 15cm returns for valances and pelmets
2 x 10cm returns for Austrian blinds

The heading and hem allowances are given at the top of the tables where appropriate. Increase or decrease these allowances as required.

Plain and Patterned Fabrics

All quantities given are for plain fabrics. These can also be used for plain lining and interlining quantities.

For patterned fabrics the cut drop needs to be adjusted to match the pattern at the seams. To do this, divide the cut drop by the length of the pattern repeat and round up the resulting figure to a whole number. Multiply this whole number by the length of the pattern repeat. This gives the adjusted cut-drop measurement.

For half-drop repeats, adjust the cut drop as above using the actual repeat measurement of the pattern, then add a further half repeat to the cut drop. The pattern will alternate at the top of each cut panel so that it will match. Number each panel and seam together in sequence.

When estimating it is useful to write down the number and length of the cut drops. It saves having to re-calculate when you are ready to cut out the fabric.

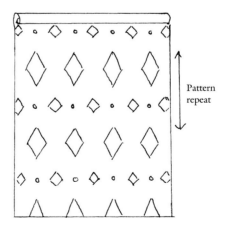

Pattern repeat

CURTAINS
2 X HEADING FULLNESS

A general heading fullness suitable for most machine heading tapes. Trimmed with contrast edges, frills and fringes there are lots of design variations to explore.

Pencil-headed curtains fixed in the centre with a Maltese cross trim.

Handy tip

Here are suggested measurements for extending the curtain track or pole either side of the window. The curtain will occupy this space when stacked back. This will allow the maximum amount of light into the room. Divide this measurement in half for a pair of curtains or use as the total stack back space for a single curtain treatment.

CURTAIN STACK BACK ALLOWANCES

Width of window	Extend track or pole by:
100–150cm	40cm
150–200cm	60cm
200–250cm	80cm
250–300cm	100cm

CURTAINS
2 X HEADING FULLNESS
30cm heading and hem allowance, 2 x 7cm overlaps and 8cm returns.
Measurements in metres.

	LENGTH OF TRACK OR POLE UP TO:								
120cm fabric	0.80	1.35	1.95	2.50	3.10	3.70	4.30	4.85	5.45
137cm fabric	0.95	1.60	2.30	2.95	3.65	4.30	4.95	5.65	6.30
150cm fabric	1.10	1.80	2.55	3.25	4.00	4.75	5.50	6.20	6.95
No. of widths	**2**	**3**	**4**	**5**	**6**	**7**	**8**	**9**	**10**
Finished length									
1.80	4.20	6.30	8.40	10.50	12.60	14.70	16.80	18.90	21.00
1.90	4.40	6.60	8.80	11.00	13.20	15.40	17.60	19.80	22.00
2.00	4.60	6.90	9.20	11.50	13.80	16.10	18.40	20.70	23.00
2.10	4.80	7.20	9.60	12.00	14.40	16.80	19.20	21.60	24.00
2.20	5.00	7.50	10.00	12.50	15.00	17.50	20.00	22.50	25.00
2.30	5.20	7.80	10.40	13.00	15.60	18.20	20.80	23.40	26.00
2.40	5.40	8.10	10.80	13.50	16.20	18.90	21.60	24.30	27.00
2.50	5.60	8.40	11.20	14.00	16.80	19.60	22.40	25.20	28.00
2.60	5.80	8.70	11.60	14.50	17.40	20.30	23.20	26.10	29.00
2.70	6.00	9.00	12.00	15.00	18.00	21.00	24.00	27.00	30.00
2.80	6.20	9.30	12.40	15.50	18.60	21.70	24.80	27.90	31.00
2.90	6.40	9.60	12.80	16.00	19.20	22.40	25.60	28.80	32.00
3.00	6.60	9.90	13.20	16.50	19.80	23.10	26.40	29.70	33.00
3.10	6.80	10.20	13.60	17.00	20.40	23.80	27.20	30.60	34.00
3.20	7.00	10.50	14.00	17.50	21.00	24.50	28.00	31.50	35.00
3.30	7.20	10.80	14.40	18.00	21.60	25.20	28.80	32.40	36.00
3.40	7.40	11.10	14.80	18.50	22.20	25.90	29.60	33.30	37.00
3.50	7.60	11.40	15.20	19.00	22.80	26.60	30.40	34.20	38.00

CURTAINS
2¼ X HEADING FULLNESS

For a fuller effect, 2¼ fullness is ideal for lots of decorative headings including hand-pleated – French and goblet, hand-gathered – trellis, pencil and smocked, puffed and slotted headings to name a few.

French-headed curtains hung from a pole.

Handy tip

See *The Encyclopædia of Curtains* pages 134-148 for ideas for decorative headings. If using a puffed heading, remember to increase the heading and hem allowance by 30-40cm to make the puffed effect. See *The Encyclopædia of Curtains* pages 135 & 137.

CURTAINS
2¼ X HEADING FULLNESS
30cm heading and hem allowance, 2 x 7cm overlaps and 2 x 8cm returns.
Measurements in metres.

	LENGTH OF TRACK OR POLE UP TO:								
120cm fabric	0.65	1.15	1.70	2.20	2.75	3.25	3.80	4.30	4.80
137cm fabric	0.80	1.40	2.00	2.60	3.20	3.80	4.35	4.95	5.60
150cm fabric	0.95	1.55	2.25	2.85	3.55	4.20	4.85	5.50	6.15
No. of widths	**2**	**3**	**4**	**5**	**6**	**7**	**8**	**9**	**10**
Finished length									
1.80	4.20	6.30	8.40	10.50	12.60	14.70	16.80	18.90	21.00
1.90	4.40	6.60	8.80	11.00	13.20	15.40	17.60	19.80	22.00
2.00	4.60	6.90	9.20	11.50	13.80	16.10	18.40	20.70	23.00
2.10	4.80	7.20	9.60	12.00	14.40	16.80	19.20	21.60	24.00
2.20	5.00	7.50	10.00	12.50	15.00	17.50	20.00	22.50	25.00
2.30	5.20	7.80	10.40	13.00	15.60	18.20	20.80	23.40	26.00
2.40	5.40	8.10	10.80	13.50	16.20	18.90	21.60	24.30	27.00
2.50	5.60	8.40	11.20	14.00	16.80	19.60	22.40	25.20	28.00
2.60	5.80	8.70	11.60	14.50	17.40	20.30	23.20	26.10	29.00
2.70	6.00	9.00	12.00	15.00	18.00	21.00	24.00	27.00	30.00
2.80	6.20	9.30	12.40	15.50	18.60	21.70	24.80	27.90	31.00
2.90	6.40	9.60	12.80	16.00	19.20	22.40	25.60	28.80	32.00
3.00	6.60	9.90	13.20	16.50	19.80	23.10	26.40	29.70	33.00
3.10	6.80	10.20	13.60	17.00	20.40	23.80	27.20	30.60	34.00
3.20	7.00	10.50	14.00	17.50	21.00	24.50	28.00	31.50	35.00
3.30	7.20	10.80	14.40	18.00	21.60	25.20	28.80	32.40	36.00
3.40	7.40	11.10	14.80	18.50	22.20	25.90	29.60	33.30	37.00
3.50	7.60	11.40	15.20	19.00	22.80	26.60	30.40	34.20	38.00

CURTAINS
2½ X HEADING FULLNESS

This is ample fullness for decorative headings. When hand pleating patterned fabrics, position the pleats over the pattern. In some cases you may need to trim away fabric at the sides of the curtain to obtain the necessary overlap and return measurements. Working to this fullness there should be sufficient fabric to do this.

Box-pleated curtains hung from a pole.

Handy tip

When using a French, goblet or box-pleated buckram heading on patterned fabrics, for a really professional finish, position the pleats over the motifs. See *The Encyclopædia of Curtains* pages 140–2 for pleat calculations and make-up instructions.

CURTAINS
2½ X HEADING FULLNESS
30cm heading and hem allowance, 2 x 7cm overlaps and 2 x 8cm returns.
Measurements in metres.

	LENGTH OF TRACK OR POLE UP TO:								
120cm fabric	0.55	1.00	1.50	1.95	2.45	2.90	3.35	3.85	4.30
137cm fabric	0.70	1.20	1.75	2.30	2.85	3.35	3.90	4.45	5.00
150cm fabric	0.80	1.40	2.00	2.55	3.15	3.75	4.35	4.90	5.50
No. of widths	**2**	**3**	**4**	**5**	**6**	**7**	**8**	**9**	**10**
Finished length									
1.80	4.20	6.30	8.40	10.50	12.60	14.70	16.80	18.90	21.00
1.90	4.40	6.60	8.80	11.00	13.20	15.40	17.60	19.80	22.00
2.00	4.60	6.90	9.20	11.50	13.80	16.10	18.40	20.70	23.00
2.10	4.80	7.20	9.60	12.00	14.40	16.80	19.20	21.60	24.00
2.20	5.00	7.50	10.00	12.50	15.00	17.50	20.00	22.50	25.00
2.30	5.20	7.80	10.40	13.00	15.60	18.20	20.80	23.40	26.00
2.40	5.40	8.10	10.80	13.50	16.20	18.90	21.60	24.30	27.00
2.50	5.60	8.40	11.20	14.00	16.80	19.60	22.40	25.20	28.00
2.60	5.80	8.70	11.60	14.50	17.40	20.30	23.20	26.10	29.00
2.70	6.00	9.00	12.00	15.00	18.00	21.00	24.00	27.00	30.00
2.80	6.20	9.30	12.40	15.50	18.60	21.70	24.80	27.90	31.00
2.90	6.40	9.60	12.80	16.00	19.20	22.40	25.60	28.80	32.00
3.00	6.60	9.90	13.20	16.50	19.80	23.10	26.40	29.70	33.00
3.10	6.80	10.20	13.60	17.00	20.40	23.80	27.20	30.60	34.00
3.20	7.00	10.50	14.00	17.50	21.00	24.50	28.00	31.50	35.00
3.30	7.20	10.80	14.40	18.00	21.60	25.20	28.80	32.40	36.00
3.40	7.40	11.10	14.80	18.50	22.20	25.90	29.60	33.30	37.00
3.50	7.60	11.40	15.20	19.00	22.80	26.60	30.40	34.20	38.00

VALANCES
2 X HEADING FULLNESS

A general heading fullness suitable for most machine heading tapes. Some tapes have a looped surface that can be fixed directly to the hook side of Velcro. Valances fitted with Velcro to the front edge of pelmet boards or valance rails have a smart taut appearance.

Gathered valance.

Handy tip for valance proportions
Fit the valance board or track up above the window and make the valance depth 1/5th or 1/6th of the curtain drop so that it just covers the top of the frame. However in rooms with low ceilings with little space above the window, the valance depth can be as little as 1/8th of the curtain drop.

VALANCES
2 X HEADING FULLNESS
15cm for heading and hem allowance,
and 2 x 15cm returns for either pelmet board or valance rail.
Measurements in metres.

LENGTH OF PELMET BOARD OR VALANCE RAIL UP TO:

120cm fabric	0.80	1.40	2.00	2.60	3.15	3.75	4.30	4.90	5.50
137cm fabric	1.00	1.65	2.30	3.00	3.65	4.35	5.00	5.70	6.35
150cm fabric	1.10	1.85	2.60	3.35	4.05	4.80	5.50	6.25	7.00
No of widths	**2**	**3**	**4**	**5**	**6**	**7**	**8**	**9**	**10**
Finished length									
0.30	0.90	1.35	1.80	2.25	2.70	3.15	3.60	4.05	4.50
0.35	1.00	1.50	2.00	2.50	3.00	3.50	4.00	4.50	5.00
0.40	1.10	1.65	2.20	2.75	3.30	3.85	4.40	4.95	5.50
0.45	1.20	1.80	2.40	3.00	3.60	4.20	4.80	5.40	6.00
0.50	1.30	1.95	2.60	3.25	3.90	4.55	5.20	5.85	6.50
0.55	1.40	2.10	2.80	3.50	4.20	4.90	5.60	6.30	7.00
0.60	1.50	2.25	3.00	3.75	4.50	5.25	6.00	6.75	7.50
0.65	1.60	2.40	3.20	4.00	4.80	5.60	6.40	7.20	8.00
0.70	1.70	2.55	3.40	4.25	5.10	5.95	6.80	7.65	8.50
0.75	1.80	2.70	3.60	4.50	5.40	6.30	7.20	8.10	9.00
0.80	1.90	2.85	3.80	4.75	5.70	6.65	7.60	8.55	9.50
0.85	2.00	3.00	4.00	5.00	6.00	7.00	8.00	9.00	10.00
0.90	2.10	3.15	4.20	5.25	6.30	7.35	8.40	9.45	10.50
0.95	2.20	3.30	4.40	5.50	6.60	7.70	8.80	9.90	11.00
1.00	2.30	3.45	4.60	5.75	6.90	8.05	9.20	10.35	11.50

VALANCES
2¼ X HEADING FULLNESS

This fullness is suitable for most types of gathered and pleated headings.

Pencil-headed serpentined shaped valance with fringe trim.

Handy tip

For arched- and serpentined-shaped valances, use the following tables to calculate the fabric quantity working to the longest measurement. To avoid the lining showing at the hem of a shaped valance, use self or contrast fabric to line the valance.

VALANCES
2¼ X HEADING FULLNESS
15cm for heading and hem allowance,
and 2 x 15cm returns for either pelmet board or valance rail.
Measurements in metres.

LENGTH OF PELMET BOARD OR VALANCE RAIL UP TO:									
120cm fabric	0.70	1.20	1.75	2.25	2.75	3.30	3.80	4.35	4.85
137cm fabric	0.85	1.45	2.05	2.65	3.20	3.85	4.40	5.00	5.60
150cm fabric	0.95	1.60	2.25	2.95	3.55	4.25	4.90	5.55	6.20
No of widths	**2**	**3**	**4**	**5**	**6**	**7**	**8**	**9**	**10**
Finished length									
0.30	0.90	1.35	1.80	2.25	2.70	3.15	3.60	4.05	4.50
0.35	1.00	1.50	2.00	2.50	3.00	3.50	4.00	4.50	5.00
0.40	1.10	1.65	2.20	2.75	3.30	3.85	4.40	4.95	5.50
0.45	1.20	1.80	2.40	3.00	3.60	4.20	4.80	5.40	6.00
0.50	1.30	1.95	2.60	3.25	3.90	4.55	5.20	5.85	6.50
0.55	1.40	2.10	2.80	3.50	4.20	4.90	5.60	6.30	7.00
0.60	1.50	2.25	3.00	3.75	4.50	5.25	6.00	6.75	7.50
0.65	1.60	2.40	3.20	4.00	4.80	5.60	6.40	7.20	8.00
0.70	1.70	2.55	3.40	4.25	5.10	5.95	6.80	7.65	8.50
0.75	1.80	2.70	3.60	4.50	5.40	6.30	7.20	8.10	9.00
0.80	1.90	2.85	3.80	4.75	5.70	6.65	7.60	8.55	9.50
0.85	2.00	3.00	4.00	5.00	6.00	7.00	8.00	9.00	10.00
0.90	2.10	3.15	4.20	5.25	6.30	7.35	8.40	9.45	10.50
0.95	2.20	3.30	4.40	5.50	6.60	7.70	8.80	9.90	11.00
1.00	2.30	3.45	4.60	5.75	6.90	8.05	9.20	10.35	11.50

VALANCES
2½ X HEADING FULLNESS

Valances can have more fullness in them than the accompanying curtains. This fullness is suitable for most decorative headings especially hand box-pleated valances (although some machine tapes require 3 x fullness) and smocked-headed valances.

Goblet-pleated valance with contrast bound hem and curtain leading edges.

Handy tip
An exciting variation for pleated valances is to make double pleats with larger scalloped spaces between. See *The Encyclopædia of Curtains* page 176-7 for make-up instructions.

VALANCES
2½ X HEADING FULLNESS
15cm for heading and hem allowance,
and 2 x 15cm returns for either pelmet board or valance rail.
Measurements in metres.

LENGTH OF PELMET BOARD OR VALANCE RAIL UP TO:								
120cm fabric	0.60	1.05	1.50	2.00	2.45	2.95	3.40	3.90	4.35
137cm fabric	0.70	1.25	1.80	2.35	2.85	3.40	3.95	4.50	5.00
150cm fabric	0.85	1.45	2.00	2.60	3.20	3.80	4.35	4.95	5.55
No of widths	**2**	**3**	**4**	**5**	**6**	**7**	**8**	**9**	**10**
Finished length									
0.30	0.90	1.35	1.80	2.25	2.70	3.15	3.60	4.05	4.50
0.35	1.00	1.50	2.00	2.50	3.00	3.50	4.00	4.50	5.00
0.40	1.10	1.65	2.20	2.75	3.30	3.85	4.40	4.95	5.50
0.45	1.20	1.80	2.40	3.00	3.60	4.20	4.80	5.40	6.00
0.50	1.30	1.95	2.60	3.25	3.90	4.55	5.20	5.85	6.50
0.55	1.40	2.10	2.80	3.50	4.20	4.90	5.60	6.30	7.00
0.60	1.50	2.25	3.00	3.75	4.50	5.25	6.00	6.75	7.50
0.65	1.60	2.40	3.20	4.00	4.80	5.60	6.40	7.20	8.00
0.70	1.70	2.55	3.40	4.25	5.10	5.95	6.80	7.65	8.50
0.75	1.80	2.70	3.60	4.50	5.40	6.30	7.20	8.10	9.00
0.80	1.90	2.85	3.80	4.75	5.70	6.65	7.60	8.55	9.50
0.85	2.00	3.00	4.00	5.00	6.00	7.00	8.00	9.00	10.00
0.90	2.10	3.15	4.20	5.25	6.30	7.35	8.40	9.45	10.50
0.95	2.20	3.30	4.40	5.50	6.60	7.70	8.80	9.90	11.00
1.00	2.30	3.45	4.60	5.75	6.90	8.05	9.20	10.35	11.50

CURVED PELMET BOARDS
FOR CURTAINS AND VALANCES

Curved pelmet boards are an attractive alternative to the standard straight board. Find out the number of widths needed and then refer to the curtain, valance and trim tables as required. Curved boards over 2m wide start to loose their curved appearance.

Puffed-headed Italian-strung curtains hung from a curved board.

More ideas

For more design ideas for curtains hung from curved boards see *The Curtain Design Directory (Third Edition)* pages 102–5 & 258–61. When curtains are hung with a valance, to follow the shape of the board, use a bay window track fitted the wrong way round (see The *Encyclopædia of Curtains* page 226).

CURVED PELMET BOARDS
2 X HEADING FULLNESS
For fixed headed curtains and valances.
For pelmet boards 30cm deep in the centre.

	Straight edge	Curved edge	Straight edge	Curved edge
120cm fabric	142cm	165cm	203cm	225cm
137cm fabric	182cm	200cm	232cm	255cm
150cm fabric	203cm	225cm	262cm	285cm
No. of widths	3		4	

CURVED PELMET BOARDS
2¼ X HEADING FULLNESS
For fixed headed curtains and valances.
For pelmet boards 30cm deep in the centre.

	Straight edge	Curved edge	Straight edge	Curved edge
120cm fabric	1.20m	1.45m	1.80m	2.00m
137cm fabric	142cm	165cm	208cm	230cm
150cm fabric	162cm	185cm	228cm	250cm
No. of widths	3		4	

CURVED PELMET BOARDS
2½ X HEADING FULLNESS
For fixed headed curtains and valances.
For pelmet boards 30cm deep in the centre.

	Straight edge	Curved edge	Straight edge	Curved edge
120cm fabric	105cm	130cm	156cm	180cm
137cm fabric	125cm	150cm	182cm	205cm
150cm fabric	142cm	165cm	203cm	225cm
No. of widths	3		4	

PELMETS

Use the longest measurement of a shaped pelmet as the finished length. Extra design details, such as rope and trumpets, can be laid on top of the pelmet to make a three dimensional effect. A lambrequin is the term given to a flat pelmet that extends either side of the window. These are often used in conjunction with a roller blind on sloping windows and skylights.

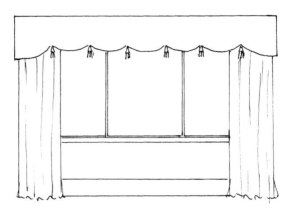

Scallop-shaped pelmet trimmed with tassels.

Skylight window with lambrequin and roller blind.

PELMETS

15cm included for top and bottom turning allowances,
2 x 15cm returns for pelmet board.
Measurements in metres.

	LENGTH OF PELMET BOARD UP TO:				
120cm fabric	1.90	3.10	4.25	5.45	6.60
137cm fabric	2.25	3.60	4.95	6.30	7.60
150cm fabric	2.50	4.00	5.45	6.95	8.40
No. of widths	**2**	**3**	**4**	**5**	**6**
Finished length					
0.30	0.90	1.35	1.80	2.25	2.70
0.35	1.00	1.50	2.00	2.50	3.00
0.40	1.10	1.65	2.20	2.75	3.30
0.45	1.20	1.80	2.40	3.00	3.60
0.50	1.30	1.95	2.60	3.25	3.90
0.55	1.40	2.10	2.80	3.50	4.20
0.60	1.50	2.25	3.00	3.75	4.50
0.65	1.60	2.40	3.20	4.00	4.80
0.70	1.70	2.55	3.40	4.25	5.10
0.75	1.80	2.70	3.60	4.50	5.40

SWAGS AND TAILS

Swags can be butted together or overlapped. A small overlap creates a pronounced scallop-shaped hemline. When swags are overlapped centre to centre, the hemline forms a shallow wavy shape.

The quantities given in the tables on pages 26–7 are based on the patterns in *The Swag and Tail Design and Pattern Book* by Merrick & Day.

Swags and tails trimmed with fringe hung from a pole.

More ideas

For more design ideas for swags and tails see *The Swag and Tail Design and Pattern Book*. It has over 70 swag designs to choose from with make-up notes and full sized swag and tail patterns. All you need to make beautiful swags and tails in one book. For even more design ideas see *The Curtain Design Directory (Third Edition)* pages 152–97.

CALCULATING SWAG WIDTHS

For overlapping swags – allow 5–20cm per overlap, i.e. increase the width of each swag by half the overlap allowance.

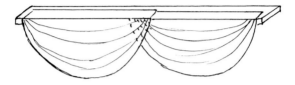

For swags butted together – divide the length of the pelmet board by the number of swags required.

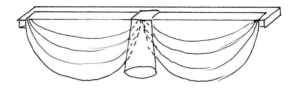

For swags wrapped over a pole – calculate as for overlapped swags and add a further 2cm to the width of each swag to allow it to bow.

SWAGS

Quantities given per swag, finished depth either 45cm or 55cm
based on patterns from *The Swag and Tail Design and Pattern Book*
by Merrick & Day. Measurements in metres.

Swag width	Fabric quantity (No. of widths x cut drop)	Hem allowance for fringe quantities
0.60	1.10 (1 x 1.10)	1.50
0.70	1.10 (1 x 1.10)	1.60
0.80	1.10 (1 x 1.10)	1.65
0.90	1.15 (1 x 1.15)	1.70
1.00	1.15 (1 x 1.15)	1.75
1.10	1.15 (1 x 1.15)	1.80
1.20	1.15 (1 x 1.15)	1.90
1.30	2.30 (2 x 1.15)	1.95
1.40	2.40 (2 x 1.20)	2.05
1.50	2.40 (2 x 1.20)	2.10
1.60	2.40 (2 x 1.20)	2.20
1.70	2.40 (2 x 1.20)	2.30

Handy tip
On plain fabrics for two or more pairs of tails, dove-
tailing the patterns will save fabric.

TAILS

Quantities given per pair, 15cm pelmet board return
based on patterns from *The Swag and Tail Design and Pattern Book*
by Merrick & Day. Measurements in metres.

Length of tail up to:	Fabric	Contrast lining	Hem measurement for fringe
0.90 – straight tail	2.00 (2 x 1.00)	2.00	2.30
1.10 – straight tail	2.40 (2 x 1.20)	2.40	2.50
1.35 – straight tail	2.90 (2 x 1.45)	2.90	3.30
1.35 – cone shape	3.30 (2 x 1.65)	3.30	3.70
1.65 – straight tail	3.50 (2 x 1.75)	3.50	3.60
1.65 – cone shape	3.90 (2 x 1.95)	3.90	4.00

Swags and tails trimmed with fringe. Rope is tacked to the
top of the pelmet board with clovers and double tassels.

SWAGGED VALANCES

Swags and trumpets are seamed together to form the valance and there is always one more trumpet than swag. To cover the ends of the pelmet board, returns are seamed onto the first and last trumpets.

To find out how many swags are needed and their size, see the table opposite. To work out the fabric requirements, ideally make the fabric and paper patterns for the valance and then measure them. Below is a table of fabric quantity suggestions based on pattern nos. 8, 9 & 10 from *The Swag and Tail Design and Pattern Book* by Merrick & Day.

Swagged valance with curtains held in tassel tie-backs.

More ideas

For more design ideas for swagged valances see *The Swag and Tail Design and Pattern Book*. It has a full sized swagged valance pattern plus make-up notes. For some more design ideas see *The Curtain Design Directory (Third Edition)* pages 190-3.

WIDTH AND NUMBER OF SWAGS

The pelmet board length includes an extra 5cm at each end of the valance
to allow the outer trumpets to sit on the front edge of the board.

Swag width	LENGTH OF PELMET BOARD		
0.60	1.30	1.90	2.50
0.70	1.50	2.20	2.90
0.80	1.70	2.50	3.30
0.90	1.90	2.80	3.70
1.00	2.10	3.10	4.10
	2 swag design	**3 swag design**	**4 swag design**

SWAGGED VALANCES

Fabric cuts	2 swags 3 trumpets	3 swags 4 trumpets	4 swags 5 trumpets
Swag cut drops	2 x 1.20	3 x 1.20	4 x 1.20
Trumpet	2 x 0.60	2 x 0.60	3 x 0.60
Returns	1 x 0.60	1 x 0.60	1 x 0.60
Fabric quantity	**4.20**	**5.40**	**7.20**

A swagged valance sewn together before pleating showing the return,
trumpet and swag sections from left to right respectively.

FINISHING TOUCHES

KNOTTED ROPE FOR PLEATED HEADINGS

Decorative rope, tied into double overhand knots, is a smart finishing touch for pleated headings. It can be hand sewn across the base of goblet, French or box pleats. Tie a length of rope, spacing the knots to fall over the centre of each pleat. Sew through the rope to the side of each knot and in the space between the pleats.

Use the curtain and valance tables to find the number of widths in your heading and look at the table opposite for suggested rope length. The rope quantities will vary according to the thickness of the rope and how loosely the knots are tied. Here the quantities are based on 12mm diameter rope, using 30cm per knot. Allow more for thicker rope.

Double overhand knot.

Handy tip

Before cutting rope, wind sticky tape around it to stop it unravelling. When stitching the rope to the curtain or valance fold the end of the rope over to the back, over sew the end and tuck it into the lining.

KNOTTED ROPE
FOR PLEATED HEADINGS 2–2½ X FULLNESS
Suggested quantities allowing 30cm per double over-hand knot
using 12mm diameter rope. Allowance made for 2 x 15cm returns.
Measurements in metres.

No. of widths	3	4	5	6	7	8	9	10
120cm fabric 4 knots/width	5.30	7.10	8.90	10.65	12.45	14.20	16.00	17.80
137cm fabric 4 knots/width	5.55	7.40	9.30	11.15	13.05	14.90	16.80	18.65
150cm fabric 5 knots/width	6.65	8.90	11.15	13.35	15.60	17.80	20.05	22.30

Goblet-headed Italian-strung curtains with rope knotted at the base of the
goblets. The centre is finished with a rope clover and double tassels.

FINISHING TOUCHES

DECORATIVE ROPE — KNOTS AND CLOVERS

Rope can be used decoratively looped, knotted and draped on top treatments to stunning effect. Rope can also be used to cover seams where yokes are joined onto valances and swags. Here are some quantity suggestions.

Arch-shaped valance set onto a flat yoke trimmed
with rope. The rope clovers are set over the trumpets.

Handy tip
When making clovers, if the rope is quite soft and
will not hold its shape, before shaping, wrap floristry
wire around it hiding the wire in the grooves.

FINISHING TOUCHES

DECORATIVE ROPE
Based on 12mm diameter rope. Allow more for thicker rope.

Knotted rope (see page 30)	Finished width including pelmet board returns + 30cm per knot + 20cm cutting allowance.
Rope clover (looped clover shape)	Finished width including pelmet board returns + 65cm per clover + 20cm cutting allowance

Swags and tails and a central trumpet, trimmed with fringe, sewn onto a flat yoke. The seam is hidden by rope, which is looped into a clover in the centre and knotted over the coronets.

FINISHING TOUCHES

GATHERED FRILLS

Frills need a surprising amount of fabric. Sometimes the quantity of fabric needed for a frill around a blind will be more than the blind itself.

GATHERED FRILLS – 2½ X FULLNESS
Frill depth 10cm, cut 23cm.
Measurements in metres.

FINISHED FRILL MEASUREMENT							
120cm fabric	1.90	2.35	2.80	3.30	3.75	4.20	4.70
137cm fabric	2.15	2.70	3.25	3.75	4.30	4.85	5.35
150cm fabric	2.35	2.95	3.55	4.15	4.70	5.30	5.90
No. of widths	**4**	**5**	**6**	**7**	**8**	**9**	**10**
Fabric quantity	**0.95**	**1.15**	**1.40**	**1.65**	**1.85**	**2.10**	**2.30**

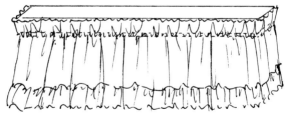

Gathered valance with a gathered frill.

Handy tip for patterned fabrics

On small pattern repeats, cut the frill strips matching the pattern. On large repeats, matching the pattern would be wasteful. Cut strips ignoring the pattern and hide the mis-matched seam in a gather.

FINISHING TOUCHES

PLEATED FRILLS

Pleated frills give a smart tailored finish. The pleats can easily be made by folding small tucks and machining them in place.

PLEATED FRILLS – 3 X FULLNESS							
Frill depth 10cm, cut 23cm. Measurements in metres.							
FINISHED FRILL MEASUREMENT							
120cm fabric	1.55	1.95	2.35	2.75	3.15	3.50	3.90
137cm fabric	1.80	2.25	2.70	3.15	3.60	4.05	4.50
150cm fabric	1.95	2.45	2.95	3.45	3.95	4.40	4.90
No. of widths	**4**	**5**	**6**	**7**	**8**	**9**	**10**
Fabric quantity	**0.95**	**1.15**	**1.40**	**1.65**	**1.85**	**2.10**	**2.30**

Goblet-headed valance with a knife pleated frill.

Handy tip

To make knife- and box-pleated frills see *The Encyclopædia of Curtains* page 157 for easy-to-use pleat templates and instructions.

FINISHING TOUCHES

PIPING AND BINDING

For decorative piping and curved contrast binding the fabric is cut at 45° to the selvedge. This is the true cross of the grain and it uses the 'give' of the fabric to allow the piping or binding to lie flat when sewn around curves.

Make piping and binding rulers from smooth timber to quickly mark out the strips.

PIPING AND CONTRAST BINDING Fabric cut on the true cross of the grain.	
Piping cut 5cm wide	0.50m will make 12.50m piping
Binding cut 8cm wide	0.50m will make 7.50m binding

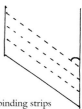

Piping or binding strips cut on the true cross.

Gathered arch-shaped valance with contrast-bound hem. The curtains are held in contrast-piped tie-backs.

Handy tip

Piping is usually cut 5cm wide. Check this width is adequate for the thickness of cord to be used. Thicker fabrics may need a thicker cord. For fabrics with a lot of stretch the strips will need to be cut wider.

FINISHING TOUCHES

FABRIC TRIMS

Fabric trims are the icing on the cake. They can be used on virtually all window treatments and look smart when used as a subtle finishing touch – trims that are too big or too bold may detract rather than complement.

FABRIC TRIMS

When using patterned fabric it is important to allow ample fabric to position the trim over a certain area of the pattern.

	Finished size	Fabric quantity
Maltese cross	10cm x 10cm	0.50m will make 2
Rosette	9cm diameter	0.50m will make 5 cut strips 8.5cm x 72cm
Coronet	10cm x 10cm	0.50m fabric, lining and stiffening will make 6
Trumpet or Decorative Tail	10cm wide at top x 40cm long	0.50m fabric and lining will make 3

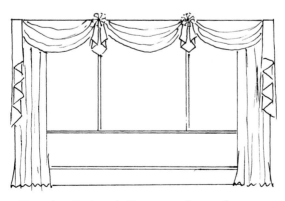

Decorative tails trimmed with rosettes set between the swags.
See page 33 for coronet and trumpet trims.

FINISHING TOUCHES

TIE-BACKS

When the curtains are fitted, hold a tape measure around them to find the correct size. The table below gives suggested measurements based on the number of widths in the curtain when hung from standard fittings. When curtains are hung in front of a radiator or at a window with a deep architrave, take account of the extra projection when choosing the size of the tie-back.

TIE-BACK SIZE CHART
Suggested measurements.

Nos of widths	Lined curtain	Interlined curtain
1-1½	50cm	60cm
1½-2	60cm	70cm
2-2½	70cm	80cm
3-3½	80cm	90cm
4-4½	90cm	100cm
5-5½	100cm	110cm
6-6½	110cm	120cm

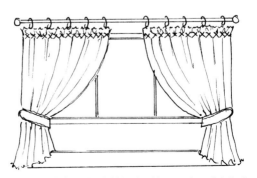

Smocked-headed curtains held in piped-banana shaped tie-backs.

FINISHING TOUCHES

TIE-BACKS
Fabric quantities per pair.

Tie-back size	Fabric, lining and stiffening quantity	No of widths x cut drop	Piping quantity
50cm or less	0.30m	1 x 0.30m	4 x embrace + 0.60m
60 – 120cm	0.60m	2 x 0.30m	4 x embrace + 0.60m

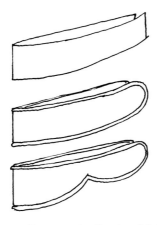

Plain, piped banana- and scallop-shaped tie-backs.

Handy tip

For quick easy-to-use patterns see *Professional Patterns for Tie-Backs* by Merrick & Day. Patterns for plain, banana- and scallop-shaped tie-backs, each in eight sizes, with clear step-by-step instructions.

ROLLER BLINDS

When fitting roller blinds inside the window reveal, to be accurate, take the measurements in millimetres.

The fabric width will be approximately 38–46mm less than the reveal size.

Pin size = reveal less 6–8mm (3–4mm each side)

Fabric width = pin size less 32–38mm (16–19mm each side). Therefore the fabric width will be 38–46mm less than reveal measurement.

ROLLER BLINDS

If stiffening fluid is to be used, this may cause the fabric to shrink in width and length so allow extra fabric. 30cm roller allowance. Measurements in metres.

	Finished width of blind up to	Finished width of blind up to
120cm fabric	1.10	2.20
137cm fabric	1.25	2.55
150cm fabric	1.35	2.80
Fabric quantity	**Finished length + 0.30**	**Finished length + 0.30 x 2**

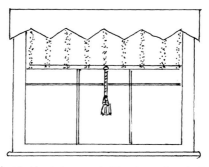

Roller blind set inside window reveal with a zig-zag shaped pelmet in front.

ROMAN BLINDS

Roman blinds can be fitted inside or outside the window reveal and are a smart form of window dressing where wall space around the window is restricted.

ROMAN BLINDS

15cm heading and hem allowance and 30cm of fabric to cover batten.
Measurements in metres.

	Finished width of blind up to	Finished width of blind up to
120cm fabric	1.10	2.20
137cm fabric	1.25	2.55
150cm fabric	1.35	2.80
Fabric quantity	**Finished length + 0.45**	**Finished length + 0.45 x 2 widths**

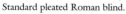

Standard pleated Roman blind.   Cascade pleated Roman blind.

More ideas

For more exciting design ideas for Roman blinds see *The Curtain Design Directory (Third Edition)* pages 208–14 and page 232.

AUSTRIAN BLINDS
2 X FULLNESS

Austrian blinds were an early form of functional drapery. With twice or less fullness and a simple gathered heading they look smart and elegant. The stringing can be set in from the sides to allow them to drop down and form small tails and the scoops give a swag effect. Braid set in from the edge is a simple but striking detail.

Gathered Austrian blind with drop-down sides.

More ideas

For more design ideas see *The Curtain Design Directory (Third Edition)* pages 216–21 & page 233.

AUSTRIAN BLINDS
2 X FULLNESS
20cm heading and hem allowance,
30cm overlong allowance and 2 x 10cm returns.
Measurements in metres.

	LENGTH OF PELMET BOARD OR RAIL UP TO:				
120cm fabric	0.90	1.50	2.10	2.70	3.25
137cm fabric	1.10	1.75	2.40	3.10	3.95
150cm fabric	1.20	1.95	2.70	3.45	4.15
No. of widths	**2**	**3**	**4**	**5**	**6**
Finished length (excl. overlong)					
1.00	3.00	4.50	6.00	7.50	9.00
1.20	3.40	5.10	6.80	8.50	10.20
1.40	3.80	5.70	7.60	9.50	11.40
1.60	4.20	6.30	8.40	10.50	12.60
1.80	4.60	6.90	9.20	11.50	13.80
2.00	5.00	7.50	10.00	12.50	15.00
2.20	5.40	8.10	10.80	13.50	16.20
2.40	5.80	8.70	11.60	14.50	17.40
2.60	6.20	9.30	12.40	15.50	18.60
2.80	6.60	9.90	13.20	16.50	19.80

AUSTRIAN BLINDS
2¼ X FULLNESS

Blinds can have almost any type of decorative heading. Pleated headings ideally need 2¼–2½ x fullness.

French-headed Austrian blind with drop-down sides.

AUSTRIAN BLINDS
2¼ X FULLNESS
20cm heading and hem allowance,
30cm overlong allowance and 2 x 10cm returns.
Measurements in metres.

	LENGTH OF PELMET BOARD OR RAIL UP TO:				
120cm fabric	0.80	1.30	1.85	2.35	2.85
137cm fabric	0.95	1.55	2.15	2.75	3.30
150cm fabric	1.05	1.70	2.35	3.05	3.65
No. of widths	**2**	**3**	**4**	**5**	**6**
Finished length (excl. overlong)					
1.00	3.00	4.50	6.00	7.50	9.00
1.20	3.40	5.10	6.80	8.50	10.20
1.40	3.80	5.70	7.60	9.50	11.40
1.60	4.20	6.30	8.40	10.50	12.60
1.80	4.60	6.90	9.20	11.50	13.80
2.00	5.00	7.50	10.00	12.50	15.00
2.20	5.40	8.10	10.80	13.50	16.20
2.40	5.80	8.70	11.60	14.50	17.40
2.60	6.20	9.30	12.40	15.50	18.60
2.80	6.60	9.90	13.20	16.50	19.80

AUSTRIAN BLINDS
2½ X FULLNESS

For a blind with ample fullness choose a light-weight fabric so that it does not become too heavy to pull up and down. For a wide window consider hanging two or more blinds next to each other.

Smocked-headed Austrian blind with drop-down sides.

Handy tip

There are many decorative headings to choose from. Gathered, smocked and various pleated headings to name a few. See *The Encyclopædia of Curtains*, Decorative Headings pages 134-43

AUSTRIAN BLINDS
2½ X FULLNESS
20cm heading and hem allowance,
30cm overlong allowance and 2 x 10cm returns.
Measurements in metres.

	LENGTH OF PELMET BOARD OR RAIL UP TO:				
120cm fabric	0.70	1.15	1.60	2.10	2.55
137cm fabric	0.80	1.35	1.90	2.45	2.95
150cm fabric	0.95	1.55	2.10	2.70	3.30
No. of widths	**2**	**3**	**4**	**5**	**6**
Finished length (excl. overlong)					
1.00	3.00	4.50	6.00	7.50	9.00
1.20	3.40	5.10	6.80	8.50	10.20
1.40	3.80	5.70	7.60	9.50	11.40
1.60	4.20	6.30	8.40	10.50	12.60
1.80	4.60	6.90	9.20	11.50	13.80
2.00	5.00	7.50	10.00	12.50	15.00
2.20	5.40	8.10	10.80	13.50	16.20
2.40	5.80	8.70	11.60	14.50	17.40
2.60	6.20	9.30	12.40	15.50	18.60
2.80	6.60	9.90	13.20	16.50	19.80

BED DRESSINGS

It is important to check the bed measurements as manufacturers' sizes vary. Listed below are the sizes used in this book.

BED SIZES			
Single	**Double**	**Queen**	**King**
90cm x 190cm	135cm x 200cm	150cm x 200cm	180cm x 200cm

BED CURTAINS

Fabric quantities for bed curtains are calculated in the same way as for window curtains.

Bed corona curtains
Allow 3 widths of fabric and contrast lining for the side curtains – 1½ widths per curtain. For the back curtain allow 2 widths of contrast lining for a single bed and 3 widths for a double bed. The side curtains can be a little overlong to allow the 'take-up' of the curtains when held in tie-backs or ombras.

Half-tester and four-poster bed curtains
Allow 2 widths of fabric and contrast lining for the side curtains – 1 width per curtain. For the back curtain allow 2 widths of contrast lining for a single bed and 3 widths for a double bed.

Decorative top treatments are calculated in the same way as window treatments. A half-tester is simply an extra wide pelmet board, up to 40cm wide x width of the bed.

CORONA BOARDS

Corona boards are semicircular pieces of wood fitted above the bed like a pelmet board and support the curtains, decorative valance, swags or pelmet as required. The table below gives suggested sizes.

BED CORONA PELMET BOARDS

Pelmet board dimensions	Back edge of board	Depth in centre of board	Curved edge measurement
Small	30cm	20cm	56cm
Medium	50cm	30cm	88cm
Large	70cm	35cm	110cm

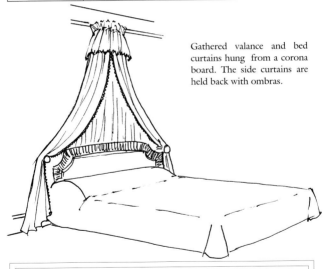

Gathered valance and bed curtains hung from a corona board. The side curtains are held back with ombras.

More ideas

For more corona bed designs see *The Curtain Design Directory (Third Edition)* pages 296–301.

BED VALANCES

Adjust allowances and quantities to suit the size of your bed. See page 48 for the bed sizes used for the table calculations.

Bed valance with a gathered skirt set into a piped seam.
Flat fabric panels set onto the lining base around three sides of the bed.

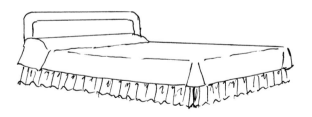

Three-quarter length bed cover set over frilled bed valance.

BED VALANCES

Frill approx 2½ x fullness, up to 40cm long, set into piped seam, fabric panels on 3 sides of the lining base. Fabric quantity includes 0.50m for piping and 0.75m (5 widths cut 15cm deep) for seamed base panels. The king-size bed has 1.50m (5 widths cut 30cm deep) for panels.

Size of bed	Fabric width	Valance frill no. of widths x cut drop	Fabric quantity	Lining quantity
Single	120cm	10 x 0.45m cut drop	**5.75m**	**6.50m**
	137cm	9 x 0.45m cut drop	**5.30m**	**6.05m**
	150cm	8 x 0.45m cut drop	**4.85m**	**5.60m**
Double	120cm	11 x 0.45m cut drop	**6.20m**	**7.05m**
	137cm	10 x 0.45m cut drop	**5.75m**	**6.60m**
	150cm	9.x 0.45m cut drop	**5.30m**	**6.15m**
Queen	120cm	12 x 0.45m cut drop	**6.65m**	**7.50m**
	137cm	10 x 0.45m cut drop	**5.75m**	**6.60m**
	150cm	9 x 0.45m cut drop	**5.30m**	**6.15m**
King	120cm	12 x 0.45m cut drop	**7.40m**	**7.50m**
	137cm	11 x 0.45m cut drop	**6.95m**	**7.05m**
	150cm	10 x 0.45m cut drop	**6.50m**	**6.60m**

Box-pleated bed valance.

Handy tip

For box pleated frills made to 3 x fullness, increase fabric and lining quantities by 3 cuts x 45cm.

UPHOLSTERED HEADBOARDS

Headboards can be made to virtually any shape, simply piped or bordered, ruched and pleated, buttoned etc.

UPHOLSTERED HEADBOARDS
Up to 80cm in height, 65cm upholstered and 15cm behind the mattress.
Measurements in metres.

Size of bed	Main Fabric	Piping	Flat border	Ruched border
Single	1.00	0.50	1.00	1.00
Double	2.00 (2 x 1.00)	0.50	1.00	2.00
Queen	2.00 (2 x 1.00)	0.75	2.00	2.00
King	2.00 (2 x 1.00)	0.75	2.00	2.00

Plain edge

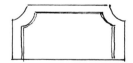

Piped flat border

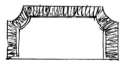

Piped with ruched border

Piped with pleated border

Design ideas
For designs for quilt stitch designs, headboards, bed covers and bed valances see *The Curtain Design Directory (Third Edition)* pages 291–3.

BED COVERS

Bed covers can be unlined, lined or lined and interlined. An unlined cover will be quite light but an interlined cover will be heavy, especially for a double bed.

Quilted covers do not crease as easily as unlined and lined covers although they are bulky to store when not in use.

BED COVERS
Quilted or lined only - full length or ¾ length.
Measurements in metres.

Size of bed	Full length width x length	¾ length width x length	Fabric and lining widths x cut drop
Single	2.05 x 2.80	1.70 x 2.65	6.40 (2 x 3.20)
Double	2.50 x 2.80	2.15 x 2.65	6.40 (2 x 3.20)
Queen	2.65 x 2.90	2.30 x 2.75	9.60 (3 x 3.20)
King	2.95 x 2.90	2.60 x 2.75	9.60 (3 x 3.20)

EXTRA DESIGN DETAILS
Measurements in metres.

Bound edge 1.50	Wadded edge 2.00	Ruched edge 3.00	Frilled edge 3.00

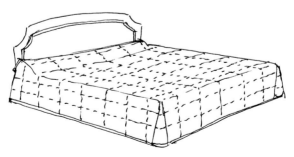

Quilted bed cover with bound edge.

ROUND TABLECLOTHS

Tablecloth diameter = table diameter + 2 x height + optional overlong allowance, usually 2–5cm.

If the cloth will need frequent washing, make it unlined and neaten the hem with a bound edge or a small hem. Lined cloths may be washed, but the lining and face fabrics may shrink by different amounts causing it not to lie flat. Interlining a table cloth gives it a luxurious padded finish and this will have to be dry cleaned. A glass top on the table will protect the cloth and keep it cleaner longer.

Round table-cloth with fringe around the hem.

Handy tip
Fabrics with a distinctive one-way pattern are not suitable for round tables as the pattern will be upside down at the back of the cloth.

ROUND TABLECLOTHS

Diameter of cloth = 2 x height of table + table top diameter
* Denotes very wasteful. The excess fabric can be used for trims
5cm hem turning allowance. Measurements in metres.

Cloth diameter up to	Fabric and lining quantity No. of widths x cut drop	Hem circumference for fringe quantities
1.70	3.60 (2 x 1.80)	5.50
1.80	3.80 (2x 1.90)	5.85
1.90	4.00 (2 x 2.00)	6.15
2.00	4.20 (2 x 2.10)	6.45
2.10	4.40 (2 x 2.20)	6.75
2.20	4.60 (2 x 2.30)	7.10
2.30	4.80 (2 x 2.40)	7.40
2.40	120cm fabric 7.50 (3 x 2.50*) 137cm fabric 5.00 (2 x 2.50) 150cm fabric 5.00 (2 x 2.50)	7.70
2.50	120cm fabric 7.80 (3 x 2.60*) 137cm fabric 5.20 (2 x 2.60) 150cm fabric 5.20 (2 x 2.60)	8.05
2.60	120cm fabric 8.10 (3 x 2.70*) 137cm fabric 5.40 (2 x 2.70*) 150cm fabric 5.40 (2 x 2.70)	8.35
2.70	120cm fabric 8.40 (3 x 2.80*) 137cm fabric 8.40 (3 x 2.80*) 150cm fabric 5.60 (2 x 2.80)	8.65
2.80	120cm fabric 8.70 (3 x 2.90*) 137cm fabric 8.70 (3 x 2.90*) 150cm fabric 5.80 (2 x 2.90)	9.00
2.90	9.00m(3 x 3.00)	9.30
3.00	9.30 (3 x 3.10)	9.60
3.10	9.60 (3 x 3.20)	9.95
3.20	9.90 (3 x 3.30)	10.20

TV AND DRESSING TABLECLOTHS

TV and dressing tablecloths are made in two pieces. A gathered skirt is hung from a track fitted to the underside of the table top. A round cloth fits on top of the table with an overhanging frill to cover the track and skirt heading.

Measure the top of the table to find the diameter and circumference. Measure from the track to the floor to find the length of the skirt.

Round TV table with frilled circular top cloth and a gathered skirt.

Handy tip
Set the skirt track 3cm in from the edge of the table top to allow the skirt to be opened and closed easily without disturbing the top cloth. Make sure the TV fits inside the table without touching the skirt.

TV AND DRESSING TABLECLOTHS

Top cloth piped with 15cm frill. Skirt 2½ x fullness, up to 75cm long,
hung from a track fitted to the underside of table top.
For round table measure the diameter, for any other shaped table
measure the circumference. Measurements in metres.

Table top diameter up to	Shaped top circumference up to	No. of widths x cut drop	Fabric and lining quantity
0.45	1.40	Top cloth 1 x 0.55 Top cloth frill 3 x 0.20 Piping 0.50 Table skirt 3 x 0.80	4.05
0.60	1.90	Top cloth 1 x 0.70 Top cloth frill 4 x 0.20 Piping 0.50 Table skirt 4 x 0.80	5.20
0.70	2.20	Top cloth 1 x 0.80 Top cloth frill 5 x 0.20 Piping 0.50 Table skirt 5 x 0.80	6.30
0.90	2.85	Top cloth 1 x 1.00 Top cloth frill 6 x 0.20 Piping 0.50 Table skirt 6 x 0.80	7.50

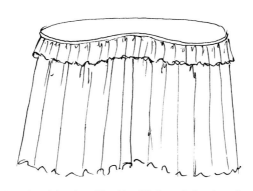

Kidney-shaped dressing table with a frilled top cloth and a gathered skirt.

CUSHIONS

Cushion covers use a relatively small amount of fabric so it's a economical way of introducing luxurious fabrics. Frilled cushions take a surprising amount of fabric and so left-over curtain fabric may not be sufficient.

For patterned fabrics allow for the repeat. This may sometimes be extremely wasteful but the pattern placement on a cushion is paramount.

SQUARE CUSHION COVERS

The cover can be made 2cm smaller than the size of the pad.

Size of cover and pad	Main fabric	Frill fabric (3 x fullness) Widths x cut drop	Fringe or piping quantities
38cm cover 40cm pad	0.50m	0.95m (4 x 0.23m)	1.70m
43cm cover 45cm pad	0.55m	0.95m (4 x 0.23m)	1.90m
48cm cover 50cm pad	0.60m	1.15m (5 x 0.23m)	2.10m
53cm cover 55cm pad	0.65m	1.15m (5 x 0.23m)	2.30m
58cm cover 60cm pad	0.70m	1.15m (5 x 0.23m)	2.50m

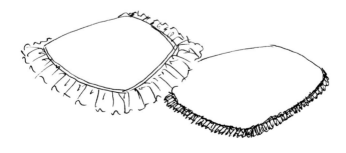

A piped and frilled cushion and a ruched trimmed cushion.

CHAIR SEAT CUSHIONS

A chair seat cushion, also known as a squab cushion, is shaped to the seat of the chair. It usually has a gusset and some form of ties to secure it to the chair. The pads can be made from feathers or foam to a depth of 5cm. Check that the height of the chair with the cushion is suitable for the table.

CHAIR CUSHION COVERS
For chairs up to 40cm deep with 5cm gusset.

Finished cover size up to:	Main fabric	Piping cord quantity	Piping fabric quantity
45cm wide x 40cm deep	0.70m	3.40m per cover	0.5m is sufficient for 3 covers

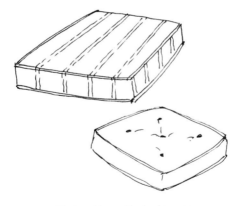

Chair cushions with piped gussets.

Handy tip
On patterned fabrics make allowances to match the front of the gusset to the pattern of the seat.

LOOSE COVERS

Make a copy of the table below to make measuring your chair or sofa quicker and easier. From these measurements calculate the fabric quantities allowing for pattern repeats as necessary.

LOOSE COVER MEASUREMENTS

Measure the width and length at the widest points.
Take extra measurements according to the shape of the chair of sofa.

Measurement	Width	Length
Outside back		
Outside arm x 2		
Inside back + tuck in		
Inside arm + tuck in x 2		
Seat + tuck in		
Lower front panel		
Gussets		
Front arm shape x 2		
Depth and type of skirt		

LOOSE COVERS

A guide for plain fabrics and patterns up to 64cm repeat.
Allow extra for larger pattern repeats.
Quantities are for average sized chairs and sofas - adjust accordingly.
Measurements in metres.

Cover description	No. of cushions	Fabric quantity	Extra fabric for small arm caps	Extra fabric for frilled/box pleated skirt
Small armchair	1	10.00	0.75	1.00
Large armchair	2	12.00	0.75	1.00
2 seater sofa	2	13.00	0.75	1.50
2 seater sofa	4	15.00	0.75	1.50
3 seater sofa	3	16.00	0.75	2.00
3 seater sofa	6	20.00	0.75	2.00

Two-seater sofa with four cushions.

GLOSSARY

ALLOWANCE
A measurement which has been added in order to turn the fabric neatly at the seams, hems or headings.

ARCHITRAVE
The wooden surround to a door or window frame.

BATTEN
A narrow length of wood used to hang blinds.

CONTRAST BINDING
Strips of contrasting fabric sewn onto edges for decorative effect.

CORNICE OR COVING
Decorative or curved moulding, usually made from plaster, fitted where the wall meets the ceiling.

CORONA
A semicircular fitting used to hang curtains above a bed. Either a semicircular track, pole or pelmet board.

CUT DROP
The cut length of fabric. It is the finished length of the curtain or top treatments with added turning allowances.

DROP PATTERN REPEAT
The measurement of a pattern which repeats itself diagonally across the width of the fabric.

FINISHED CURTAIN LENGTH
The length of the curtain when ready to hang.

FULLNESS RATIO
The relationship between the track or pelmet board measurement and the width of the ungathered curtain or valance.

HEADING
The way in which the top of the curtain, valance etc. is finished in a decorative way.

LAMBREQUIN
A pelmet with deep sides which can extend to the floor.

ONE–WAY DESIGN
Fabric with a pattern or weave going in one direction as opposed to a two-way design.

OVERLAP ARMS
Extentions of corded tracks which let the curtains cross over in the centre.

OVERLAP ALLOWANCE
Extra width to allow a pair of curtains to cross over in the centre to exclude light and draughts.

OVERLONG
Extra length to allow the curtains to lie on the floor. Also referred to as puddling on the floor.

GLOSSARY

PATTERN REPEAT
The length of the pattern before it repeats itself.

PELMET
A fabric covered band of buckram or ply-wood which is fixed around a pelmet board. It conceals the curtain track and heading.

PELMET BOARD
A piece of planed timber fixed to the wall like a shelf, used to support curtain track, valance, swags and tails etc.

PIPING
Cord sandwiched inside a strip of fabric, usually cut on the true cross and often in a contrasting colour, inserted into a seam.

RETURN
The space between the front of the window treatment and the wall. This is covered for neatness and to exclude light and draughts.

Curtain return – The outside edge which turns the corner from the face of the track to the wall.

Pelmet board return – The measurement from the front of the board to the wall, covered by the pelmet or valance return.

STACK BACK
The wall area at the side of the window covered by the curtain. The curtain 'stacks back' or folds into this area when opened.

STIFFENING
Stiff fabric used inside flat pelmets and tie-backs.

TESTER
A full canopy over a four poster bed. A half-tester is a rectangular pelmet board or curtain rail above a bed.

TRACK
A metal or plastic rail from which the curtain is hung on gliders.

TRUE CROSS OF THE GRAIN
A line at 45° to the selvedge of the fabric.

VALANCE
A gathered band of fabric hung from the front edge of a pelmet board or valance rail. It hides the track and curtain heading. A valance is a gathered equivalent of a flat pelmet.

WINDOW RECESS
The area inside the reveal of the window where blinds and sheer curtains can be fitted.

NOTES